Illinois Fish Species

Game Fish & Panfish

Billy Grinslott & Kinsey Marie Books

ISBN - 9781965098813

The Green Sunfish is blue green in color. It has yellow flecks on both its scales and some parts of its sides. The Green Sunfish also has broken blue stripes which is why some people confuse it with the Bluegill. Green Sunfish are very adaptable, they can live in any body of water that has vegetation or weeds. Green sunfish are opportunistic feeders, consuming insects, small fish, and other invertebrates.

Longear sunfish are small, thin-bodied fish with a unique long ear flap on their gill cover, that how they got their name long ear. They are often mistaken for a pumpkinseed. They have an olive to rusty-brown back, a bright orange belly. They typically reach a length of 4.5 inches. They are mostly active during the day and inactive at night.

Bantam sunfish are known for their dusky olive coloration with rows of dark spots along their sides and faint, irregular vertical bars. They are small, robust sunfish, with a maximum size of 4 inches. They are found in swamps, mud-bottomed and heavily vegetated ponds, lakes, and sloughs. They are primarily found in the western Mississippi River lowlands, from southern Illinois to Texas.

Redear sunfish are known for their red or orange-edged gill flaps. They are a type of sunfish that thrive in warm, quiet waters, feeding primarily on mollusks and snails, and can grow up to 12 inches and weigh as much as 2 pounds. They are also known as shellcracker, due to their diet and the way they crush shells. The redear sunfish will thrive in most warm-water lakes and streams.

The Warmouth is a member of the Rock Bass, Green Sunfish and Bluegill family. They can survive in low oxygen environments while other fish cannot. Warmouth can thrive in muddy water, when other fish can't. Warmouth are often confused with rock bass. The difference between the two is in the anal fin: warmouth have three spines on the anal fin ray and rock bass have six spines.

Redhorse fishes are part of the sucker family and are known for their bottom-facing mouths and fleshy lips which they use to suck food off the bottom. Redhorse has large, molar-like throat teeth that are an adaptation for crushing the shells of mollusks. redhorses construct nests in clean gravel, using their tails to sweep and their mouths to carry rocks or move materials with their heads.

The bluegill also considered a sunfish is the most popular fish to fish for. They are called pan fish because they are about the size of a frying pan. Bluegills love to eat insects and bugs. They have good vision and rely on their keen eyesight to feed. Three types in this group are the Bluegill, Sunfish, and Pumpkinseed.

The Pumpkinseed is also known as pond perch, sun perch, and punky's sunfish. It can be found in numerous lakes, ponds, and rivers. It is their body shape resembling the seed of a pumpkin, that inspired their name. Pumpkinseed sunfish have speckles on their orangish colored sides and back, with a yellow to orange belly and chest. They are active during the day and rest at night near the bottom or in shelter areas.

The two most famous perches are the common perch and the yellow perch. The yellow perch has a brilliant greenish yellow color with orange fins. The yellow perch is the biggest one and can grow to a size of 18 inches. It's also known as the jumbo perch. The other type of perch is the white perch.

The Rock Bass is not actually a bass but a member of the sunfish family. The biggest Rock Bass ever caught on record weighs about three pounds and was a little over one foot long. Rock bass like waters with rocky vegetated areas, that's how they got their name.

There are two main types of crappies. The white crappie and the black crappie. They are also members of the sunfish family. The difference between the white and black crappie is one has dark spots and the other has dark lines and is lighter in color. The white crappie has six dorsal fin spines, whereas the black crappie has eight dorsal fin spines. The white crappie can grow bigger and more of the bigger white crappie are caught in North America.

The sucker fish has the same mouth as a carp. They got their name because their mouth is like a suction cup. They normally are bottom feeders and suck their food from the bottom of the lake. Many people use sucker fish to fish for northern pike and other big game fish.

Flathead Catfish, their body is wide but flattened and very low in height. Both eyes are on the top of the flattened head, giving excellent vision to see upward. Flathead catfish live mainly in large bodies of water like big rivers and reservoirs. They prefer deep pools. The largest flathead catfish caught in Illinois weighed 81.4 pounds.

The black bullhead and yellow bullhead are part of the catfish family. They usually only grow to about 10 inches long. They use their whiskers to help find food. The bullhead is the most common member of the catfish family. Bullheads live in the water containing low oxygen levels. They can survive on low oxygen areas, where other fish can't.

There are several species of catfish. The Channel Catfish are the most fished catfish species with around 8 million anglers fishing for them per year. Blue catfish are known for their size, reaching over 100 pounds. Blue catfish, like other catfish, lack scales and have smooth skin. They have barbels (whiskers) around their mouths, which are used for sensing and tasting food. They are generally slate blue on the back and silvery/white on the underside. The largest blue catfish ever caught in Illinois weighed 124 pounds.

Bowfins can breathe both air and water, putting them at an advantage in low-oxygen waters. Bowfins are often described as prehistoric relics. This is because species can be traced to fossils from the Cretaceous, Eocene and Jurassic period. The largest bowfin caught in Illinois, by hook and line, weighed 16 pounds and 6 ounces.

White Bass range in color from a silvery white to a pale green. Their backs are mostly black, while their sides and belly are pale with stripes running along them. White Bass are related to Striped Bass and called wipers. The largest white bass caught in Illinois weighed 4 pounds and 14 ounces.

Striped bass are often called Stripers. Striped bass live in both salt and fresh water. Striped bass have very sensitive eyes and will seek deep water when the sun is out. Striped bass have a preferred water temperature range of from 55° F to 68° F, and swim to find water of these temperatures. Striped bass can grow up to 5 feet long and weigh up to 77 pounds. The largest recorded striped bass was 125 pounds and was caught in 1891. The largest striped bass caught in Illinois weighed 31 pounds and 7 ounces,

Yellow bass, scientifically known as Morone mississippiensis, are a relatively small, schooling fish with a golden-yellow body and dark stripes, often found in rivers and lakes, particularly in areas with dense vegetation. The average size for this fish is 12 inches in length and one pound in weight. They are also known as rockfish, streaker, and yellow belly. The largest yellow bass caught in Illinois weighed 2 pounds.

There are few different species of Gar, the Longnose gar, Short nose and spotted gar. The Gar got its name because of its long mouth that looks like an alligator's mouth. The alligator gar is one of the biggest freshwater fish growing up to 10 feet long. The world record for a catch was set at 327 pounds. The largest longnose gar caught in Illinois by hook and line weighed 22 pounds and 1 ounce.

Lake Sturgeons have sharp spines on their back, so be careful when handling them. Instead of scales, sturgeon skin is covered in bony plates called scutes, which can be very sharp on young sturgeon. Sturgeons have been around since the dinosaur days. Sturgeons mostly live in large, freshwater lakes and rivers. Their average lifespan is 50 to 60 years. The largest sturgeon ever caught in Illinois was a lake sturgeon, weighing 310 pounds and measuring seven feet, 11 inches long.

The burbot, also known as the eel pout. They get their name because they have a serpent-like or eel-like body. They can wrap their tail around things. There's nothing to worry about if you catch one, they may try to wrap their tail around your arm, but they are harmless. Burbots are adapted to cold water and are found in large, cold rivers, lakes, and reservoirs, primarily preferring freshwater habitats. Burbots are also known as eelpout, lingcod, and lawyer. The largest burbot caught in Illinois weighed 11 pounds, 12.5 ounces, Length 33 inches.

Male freshwater drum make a rumbling or grunting sound by contracting muscles along their air bladder walls. They have large, ivory-like ear bones that can be up to an inch in diameter, which Native Americans used as necklaces or bracelets and sometimes referred to as the lucky stones. Freshwater drum are primarily bottom feeders, spending much of their time near the bottom of lakes and rivers in search of food. The largest freshwater drum caught in Illinois weighed 38 pounds and 4 ounces.

Buffalo Fish are sometimes confused with carp. Buffalo fish have a downward-facing mouth, capable of sucking bits of food out of the silt and sand on the bottom. They have broad bodies, blunt heads, and silvery gray or brown scales. Buffalo fish are members of the suckerfish family. The largest buffalo fish caught in Illinois, specifically a bigmouth buffalo, weighed 48 pounds.

Carp have long been an important food fish to humans. Carp are bottom feeders for the most part and their mouth is made like a suction cup, so they can suck food off the bottom. Carp are good for a lake because they help clean the bottom of the lake. The largest carp caught in Illinois was a bighead carp, weighing in at a massive 109 pounds.

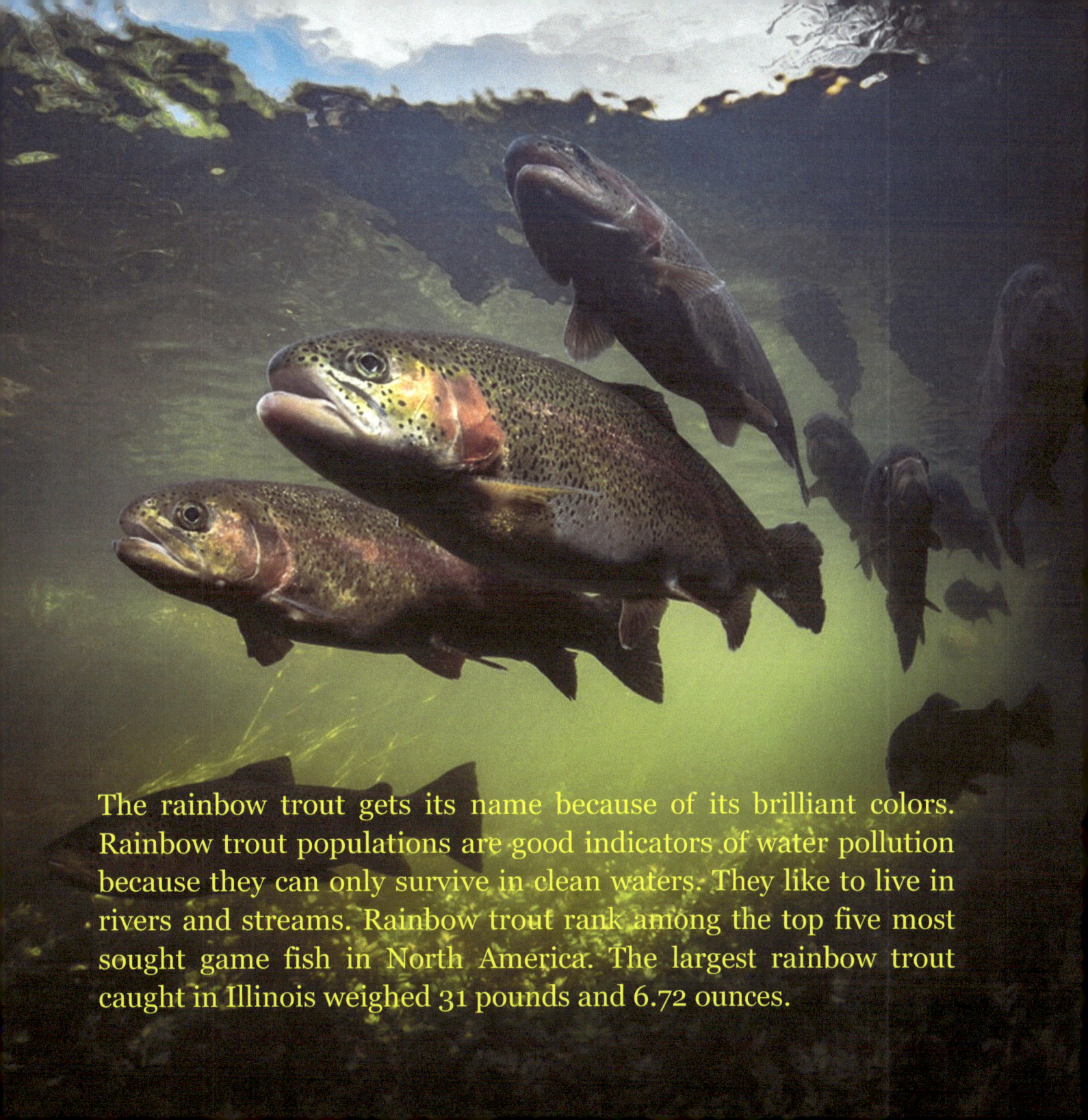

The rainbow trout gets its name because of its brilliant colors. Rainbow trout populations are good indicators of water pollution because they can only survive in clean waters. They like to live in rivers and streams. Rainbow trout rank among the top five most sought game fish in North America. The largest rainbow trout caught in Illinois weighed 31 pounds and 6.72 ounces.

The lake trout is one of the biggest of the trout family. The biggest lake trout caught was 72 pounds. Lake trout like to live in lakes that are deep. They like being in the cool water in the deep parts of a lake. They have been reported to live up to 70 years in some Canadian lakes. The largest lake trout caught in Illinois weighed 39.16 pounds, It was 45 1/2 inches long.

Chinook also known as the king salmon are the most widespread Salmon in North America. Chinook salmon are hatch in freshwater streams and rivers then migrate out to the saltwater environment of the ocean to feed and grow. Chinook salmon are the largest of the Pacific Ocean salmon, that's how they got the name king salmon. The largest Chinook (King) salmon caught in Illinois weighed 37 pounds.

Coho salmon, also known as silver salmon, are fish that live in both freshwater and saltwater, migrating from the ocean to their natal streams to spawn, where they die shortly after. Some coho salmon migrate more than 1,000 miles in the ocean, while others remain in marine areas close to the streams where they were born. Adult coho salmon typically weigh 8 to 12 pounds and are 24 to 30 inches long, but some can reach up to 36 pounds. The largest coho salmon caught in Illinois weighed 20 pounds and 9 ounces.

Pink salmon have the shortest lifespan of any salmon. Male pink salmon develop a distinct hump on their backs, which is why they're sometimes called humpies. They are the smallest of the salmon species, averaging between 3 and 6 pounds. Pink salmon return to the same stream or river where they were born to spawn. Pink salmon are found throughout the cold waters in lake Michigan. The largest pink salmon caught in Illinois weighed 4.9 pounds and was 23.5 inches long.

Spotted bass have rows of dark spots on their sides and an iridescent green pattern along their back. Spotted bass are also known as Kentucky's or redeye bass. They are a popular game fish, often mistaken for largemouth bass, but they have subtle differences like a a smaller mouth. They are known for their aggressive nature and tendency to school together. They also prefer rocky bottoms and being in deeper water compared to other bass who like shallow water. The largest spotted bass caught in Illinois weighed 7 pounds and 3 ounces.

Smallmouth bass have a smaller mouth than the largemouth bass. They also have different markings and are lighter in color. They don't live in most lakes because they prefer living in colder water. They are typically found in the northern states in America because the water is cooler. The current world record smallmouth is an 11-pound, 15-ounce fish caught in Dale Hollow Lake. The largest smallmouth bass caught in Illinois weighs 7 pounds and 3 ounces, Length 22 1/4 inches.

The largemouth bass is the most sought-after bass in North America. Largemouth bass live in just about every lake in North America. They have great hearing and can hear a crayfish crawling on the bottom of the lake. The largest largemouth bass caught in Illinois weighed 13 pounds and 1 ounce.

The sauger is part of the walleye family. There are 2 different types of saugers. The normal sauger and the suageye. The saugeye is a mix of the sauger and walleye. The suageye have white eyes just like the walleye. The sauger and suageye are smaller than the walleye. Saugers are more likely to be found in large rivers with deep pools but are also found in lakes. The largest sauger caught in Illinois weighed 5 pounds, 12.5 ounces.

The walleye got its name because of its white looking eyes. Their eyes collect light, even in low light conditions. This means they can see in the dark. Because they can see in the dark, they mostly feed at night. During the daytime their eyes are very sensitive, so they usually head for deeper water or shady places. Walleye like to live in cooler water and are normally found in the upper part of North America. The largest walleye caught in Illinois, weighing in at 15.08 pounds and measuring 31.5 inches long.

The Northern Pike is one of the most sought-after fish for anglers. It got its name because it likes to live in cooler water mainly in the northern states of North America. The northern pike is a very aggressive predator. They don't like to live in groups with other fish, they are very territorial and like to live alone. Their behavior is closely affected by weather conditions. The largest Northern Pike caught in Illinois weighed 26 pounds and 15 ounces.

The muskellunge called the Musky or Muskie for short is one of the biggest game fish in freshwater lakes. The largest on record was 69 pounds, 15 ounces. The Muskie likes to live in cooler water and can be found in most lakes in the upper part of north America. Anglers look at Muskellunges as trophy fish. They are hard to catch, there's a saying that it takes a thousand casts to catch one. The largest muskellunge caught in Illinois weighed 38 pounds, 8 ounces, Length 50 3/4 inches.

Fun Facts About Illinois Fish

1 - The bluegill was elected the State Fish in 1986 by Illinois schoolchildren. Its name refers to Its bright blue gill covers.

2 - Illinois has 30 families of fish, 203 species of fish, with 180 being native and 16 introduced.

3 - The lake sturgeon is a giant, with some weighing over 100 pounds and living over 150 years.

4 - Largemouth bass are the most common fish in Illinois for anglers to pursue.

5 - Salmon were introduced to Lake Michigan as early as 1800 and the lake still holds a good populations.

6 - The burbot, also known as eelpout, is a member of the freshwater cod family and has an odd habit of wrapping its slimy tails around the hand or arm of anglers.

7 - Panfish are caught most frequently followed by bass.

Author Page

Billy Grinslott & Kinsey Marie Books

Copyright, All Rights Reserved

ISBN – 9781965098813

Thanks